Be My Neighbor

Maya Ajmera & John D. Ivanko
with words of wisdom from Fred Rogers

USA

Charlesbridge

W9-BON-886

Words of Wisdom from Fred Rogers

On our television program, *Mister Rogers' Neighborhood,* I sing, "Won't you be my neighbor?" Neighbors are people who care about and help each other. Sometimes they live in the same real neighborhood. But they can also be "neighbors" even if they live far away. They might live in a different country, where people talk differently or wear different clothes or eat different foods, but they can still be our "neighbors." They can still be people we care about, just because they're human beings.

Every person in this world started out as a baby needing food and diapers and a place to sleep and most of all—love. In fact, every person started out just like you. As different as we are from one another, as unique as each one of us is, we are much more the same than we are different.

—Fred Rogers (1928-2003)

Generously shared by Family Communications, Inc.,
the nonprofit company founded by Fred Rogers.

Israel

Your neighborhood is a special place.

Papua New Guinea

A neighborhood is where you live, learn, grow up, play, and work, surrounded by your family and friends. Each and every neighborhood is a special place. Yours might be in the mountains, along a coast, or somewhere in between. It might have important historical sites, such as a monument or the home of someone famous.

Oman

Spain

It may be part of a village, town, or big city.

China

Canada

USA

Neighborhoods around the world can look very different. Some neighborhoods have lots and lots of people in them, while others have only a small population, such as those on a remote island, in the country, or high up in the hills. Some neighborhoods are made up of a few buildings in a town or village, while others stretch for miles and miles and are part of a big city.

South Africa

Every neighborhood is made up of lots of different people . . .

Your neighborhood can be made up of people of all ages, interests, and backgrounds. Some members of your neighborhood may live like you and your family, and others may have different habits and customs that are celebrated in different kinds of festivals and community activities. The post office, town square, places of worship, and sports fields are places where people from your community come together.

Mexico

USA

Vietnam

. . . and lots of different homes.

A house can be just for your family or it can be an apartment in a large building where many families live next to one another. Houses can be made from different materials, such as wood, brick, glass, or even mud, grass, or rocks. In places where the weather is cold, houses are made to keep you warm. In warm climates houses are built to keep you cool. No matter where you live, houses are for making you and your family comfortable, dry, and safe.

Philippines

Japan

Mongolia

Mali

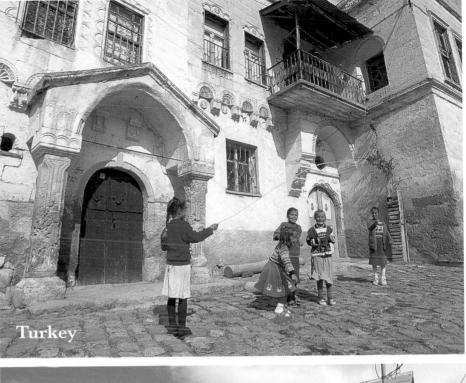

Turkey

Bahamas

Neighborhoods also have schools . . .

Mauritania

Kenya

Brazil

There are many kinds of schools in your neighborhood. Some are large, and some may be as small as just one room. Sometimes school is held in your house. Schools are important because they help you learn and become more helpful to your community.

China

Cuba

. . . places to worship . . .

Thailand

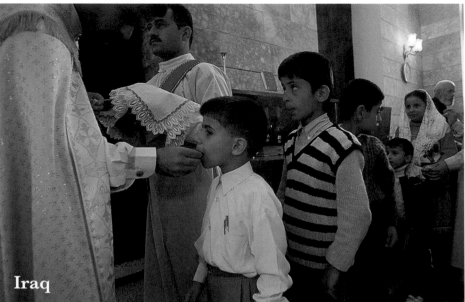

Iraq

Brunei

Jamaica

USA

Your neighborhood often has one or more places to worship, depending on the religious beliefs of the people who live there. You might go with your family to a large cathedral, synagogue, or mosque. You may have friends who go to a temple or worship in their home.

. . . places to play . . .

Mexico

France

Parks, plazas, streets, and backyards are all places to play in a community. If your neighborhood is near a lake, a river, or an ocean, you and your friends might go swimming, fishing, or boating. Swimming pools, ice rinks, sports fields, and playgrounds are places especially made for having fun.

USA

Belize

Mexico

Many neighborhoods have markets, restaurants, shopping malls, or grocery stores to buy what you and your family need. Some places are large with lots of different things for sale, while other stores are small, selling only specific items like bread or cheese. You can even create your own place to sell something homemade to others in your community.

. . . and places to buy the things you need.

France

USA

USA

Costa Rica

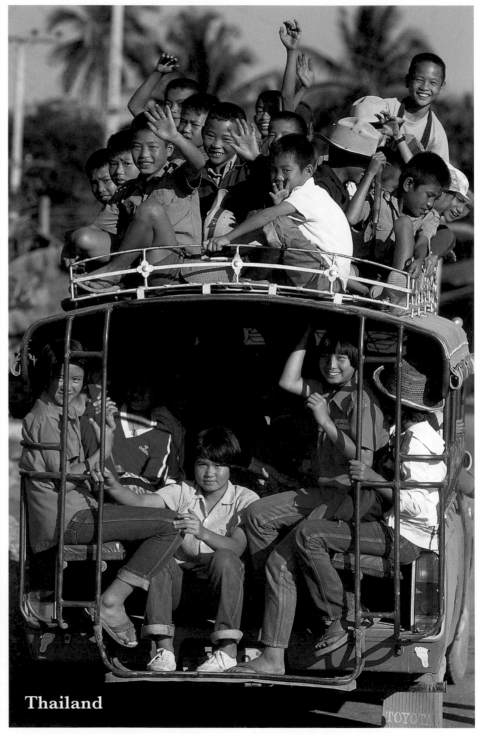

Thailand

There are lots of ways to get around your neighborhood.

Buses, cars, trains, boats, and big trucks are some ways that you can get from one part of your neighborhood to another. For short distances, walking, biking, or skateboarding are also good ways to get around with your friends. By sharing rides or using public transportation, you meet other people who live in, work in, or visit your neighborhood.

Argentina

India

USA

India

Russia

Neighborhoods have special events and big celebrations.

Special events such as anniversaries, block parties, or local festivals let you join other people in your community to celebrate and to share in some fun and great food. Parades, cultural events, and national holidays are other big celebrations that bring a neighborhood together.

Spain

In your neighborhood you share responsibilities . . .

USA

Japan

USA

Denmark

United Kingdom

People who live in the same neighborhood often work together to make it a better place. You might join your neighbors to clean up a river or work with a youth group to plant trees in a park. Neighbors look out for one another, perhaps helping someone find a lost dog or picking up fallen branches after a big storm. There are also people in your neighborhood whose job it is to take care of you: doctors, police officers, firefighters, and mail carriers, for example.

. . . and help out your family and friends.

China

Somalia

Your family often counts on your help, perhaps with growing fruits and vegetables to sell at the market or taking care of the lawn when you are old enough. Babysitting, feeding neighbors' pets while they are out of town, or reading with an elderly person are neighborly ways of helping other people.

India

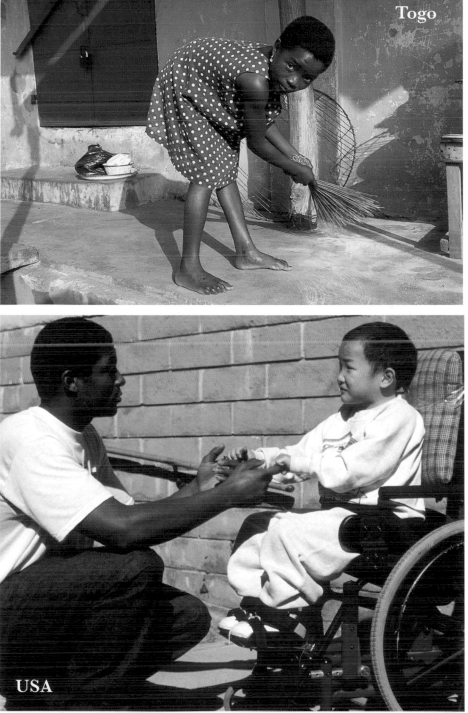

Togo

USA

Your neighborhood is where you feel at home.

Neighbors have in common the place where they live. You celebrate your neighborhood because you're a part of it and it's a part of you. Your neighborhood is a place where you learn about cooperation, respect, and friendship. It's the place you call home.

Romania

South Africa

Guatemala

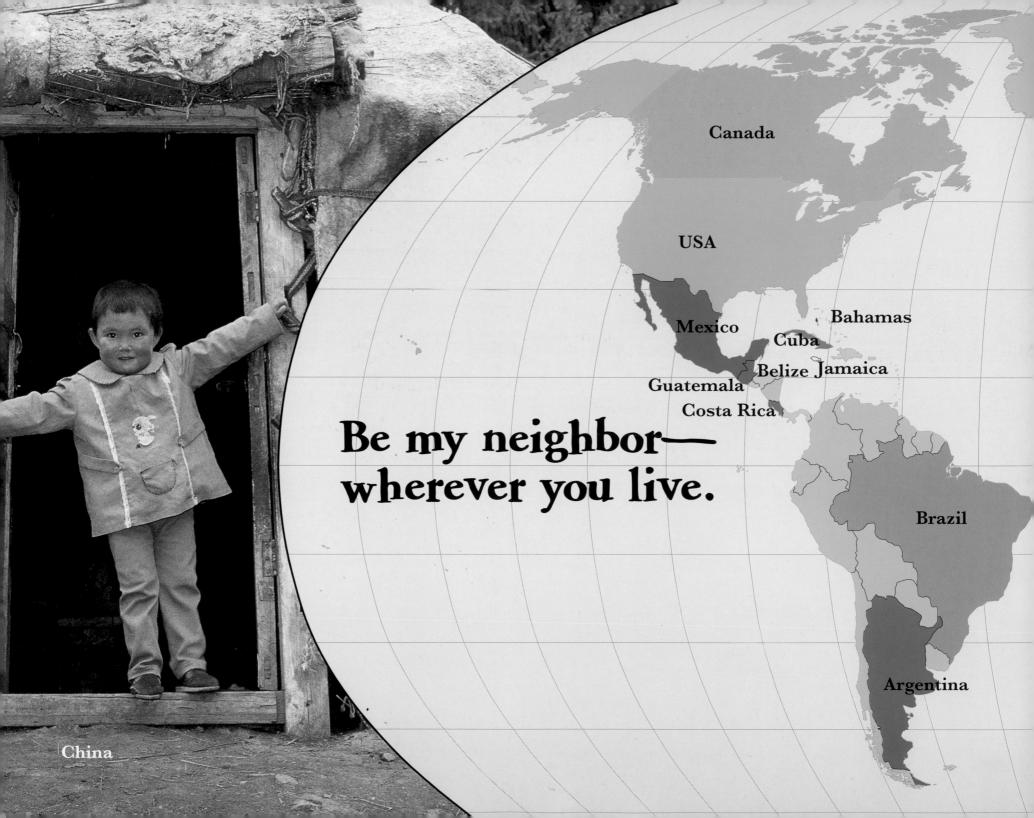

Canada

USA

Mexico

Bahamas

Cuba

Belize Jamaica

Guatemala

Costa Rica

Be my neighbor—
wherever you live.

Brazil

Argentina

China

Be My Neighbor is dedicated to Children's Town, Malambanyama Village, Zambia.—M. A.

For the "seventh generation of children on earth."—J. D. I.

Be My Neighbor was developed by the Global Fund for Children, a nonprofit organization committed to advancing the dignity of children and youth around the world. Global Fund for Children books teach young people to value diversity and help them become productive and caring global citizens. Visit www.globalfundforchildren.org to learn more about Children's Town in Zambia.

Developed by Global Fund for Children Books
1101 Fourteenth Street, NW, Suite 420
Washington, DC 20005
(202) 331-9003
www.globalfundforchildren.org

Published by Charlesbridge
85 Main Street
Watertown, MA 02472
(617) 926-0329
www.charlesbridge.com

Details about the donation of royalties can be obtained by writing to Charlesbridge Publishing and the Global Fund for Children.

Library of Congress Cataloging-in-Publication Data
Ajmera, Maya.
  Be my neighbor / Maya Ajmera and John D. Ivanko.
  p. cm.
  Summary: A simple introduction to the characteristics of a neighborhood.
  ISBN-13: 978-1-57091-504-8; ISBN-10: 1-57091-504-0 (reinforced for library use)
  ISBN-13: 978-1-57091-685-4; ISBN-10: 1-57091-685-3 (softcover)
1. Neighborhood—Juvenile literature. 2. Community—Juvenile literature. 3. Child volunteers—Juvenile literature. [1. Neighborhood. 2. Community.] I. Ivanko, John D. (John Duane), 1966- . II. Title.
HM756.A36 2004
307.3'362—dc22
2003021230

Printed in Korea
(hc) 10 9 8 7 6 5
(sc) 10 9 8 7 6 5 4

Display type and text type set in P22 Garamouche and Monotype Baskerville
Color separated, printed, and bound by Sung In Printing, South Korea

I want to thank John Ivanko for a wonderful partnership for many years. In addition, thank you to Cynthia Pon, Joan Shifrin, and Kelly Swanson Turner for their creative insights.
    —Maya Ajmera

Thanks to my ever-cheering wife, Lisa Kivirist, and son, Liam Ivanko Kivirist, and especially my mom, Susan Ivanko, who unselfishly demonstrates what being a good neighbor means, every day. It's always such a pleasure to be creative with Maya Ajmera and share in her vision for what the world can become, one child, and neighborhood, at a time.

    —John Ivanko

We would like to thank all the photographers who contributed to this wonderful book. Without their vision, we would have no book. We are grateful to Bill Isler and his team at Family Communications, Inc., who graciously shared the words of wisdom from Fred Rogers. We want to thank the Flora Family Foundation, the W. K. Kellogg Foundation, and the Arie and Ida Crown Memorial for their financial support to develop this book.